Deciphering

curious directive

methuen | drama

LONDON • NEW YORK • OXFORD • NEW DELHI • SYDNEY

METHUEN DRAMA

Bloomsbury Publishing Plc, 50 Bedford Square, London, WC1B 3DP, UK
Bloomsbury Publishing Inc, 1359 Broadway, New York, NY 10018, USA
Bloomsbury Publishing Ireland, 29 Earlsfort Terrace, Dublin 2,
D02 AY28, Ireland

BLOOMSBURY, METHUEN DRAMA and the Methuen
Drama logo are trademarks of Bloomsbury Publishing Plc.

First published in Great Britain 2025

Cover image by Guy Sanders

Bloomsbury Publishing Plc does not have any control over, or responsibility
for, any third-party websites referred to or in this book. All internet addresses
given in this book were correct at the time of going to press. The author and
publisher regret any inconvenience caused if addresses have changed or sites
have ceased to exist, but can accept no responsibility for any such changes.

No rights in incidental music or songs contained in the work are hereby
granted and performance rights for any performance/presentation
whatsoever must be obtained from the respective copyright owners.

All rights whatsoever in this play are strictly reserved and application
for performance etc. should be made before rehearsals begin to the author
via Bloomsbury Publishing, performance.permissions@bloomsbury.com.
No performance may be given unless a licence has been obtained.

A catalogue record for this book is available from the British Library.

A catalog record for this book is available from the Library of Congress.

ISBN: PB: 978-1-3506-0638-8
ePDF: 978-1-3506-0639-5
eBook: 978-1-3506-0640-1

Series: Modern Plays

Typeset by Mark Heslington Ltd, Scarborough, North Yorkshire

For product safety related questions contact
productsafety@bloomsbury.com.

To find out more about our authors and books visit
www.bloomsbury.com and sign up for our newsletters.

DECIPHERING

by curious directive

19th December 2017, 5:55am.

On a sub-zero December morning, I find myself sat on a wooden bench in The Lot, Dordogne, France. These benches are numbered, optimistically, 1-50 for prospective visitors of Font-de-Gaume, a polychromatic cave system. I'm sat on number one. A light switches on in an office nearby. An official unlocks the door, and asks me (in French) if I'm here to see the cave. I nod. I've arrived early, keen not to miss my chance. It turns out that visiting polychromatic caves are more of a summer activity here. Which makes sense. Up the road is the world-famous Lascaux, but I'm intrigued by something smaller, something more intimate.

It's now 8am. The guided tour is about to start, and I'm joined by a friendly, elderly couple from New Zealand and a Spanish archaeologist who hastily arrived by motorbike. We meet Severine, a calm high priestess of a tour guide, and we begin to the climb the slope up to the entrance of the Font-de-Gaume – one of the only remaining polychromatic caves open to the general public.

We approach the entrance of the cave, a large iron door is opened and we begin our first steps down a suspended walkway, flanked by dim festoons, into a chamber. The temperature has warmed significantly. We are asked to face a wall, and let our eyes adjust. Then, after around 30 seconds, the hind of an animal appears. It's a bison. Etched onto the wall during the Upper Palaeolithic period (17,000 years ago). We all witness, in stillness, this expression of artistry. Severine, our guide, then turns to show us a negative handprint. It's a stencil. A child's hand in rich, red ochre. And, impossibly, this tiny hand is 6ft in the air. There are no rocks below to climb up and yet, this tiny hand, is marked on the wall. How did this child's hand scale the wall like this? This was the starting point for *Deciphering*. This was when I knew I'd make a play about cave symbols.

1st July 2020, 9am

I'm waiting to speak to actor Stephanie Street. We've all had a strange time since March. Theatre has been shut down, artists haven't worked. I speak with Steph, whom I've known for a number of years, about an idea for a show which includes a mother and a daughter. Her daughter, Asha is seven at the time. We discuss what it might be like to try to workshop a story about a mother and daughter, exploring cave paintings and education. Steph agrees that we should spend a few weeks together at our making space in Norwich to explore the play.

12th August – 21st August 2020

Steph and Asha join us in Norwich, alongside a stellar devising company. Initially we explore the Northern Spanish caves (as we have two Spanish speakers with us). We explore a teacher character, but most importantly we re-connect with each other as artists. The idea of a character, Elise, who is 8 years old emerges. The idea that we see this 8-year-old as a 25-year-old and again (in the present day) as a 48-year-old is solidified. So the mother/daughter collaboration becomes about two biologically connected artists playing themselves at different ages. The expanse of one life feels very important. We consider a portacabin classroom; we dream of the floor being on a hydraulic lift, enabling the actors to descend into a cave system. David Byrne, from New Diorama Theatre (at the time), confirms the work will be programmed. Exactly when, we cannot fully know. As we crash down to earth from this dream-like process, another lockdown is announced.

9th September – 18th October 2021

Our final assembled team crosses continents. With the primary school now set in Jakarta, Indonesia, we collaborate with the sound artists Bombo (based in Makassar) as well as introducing the extraordinary Faizal Abdullah into the creative team, who in turn introduces Bahasa into the spoken language of the show - this is rare in British theatre. The story now spans from France to rural Indonesia. Tethered by a storyline of Elise, an 8-year-old, and a day in the classroom with her new teacher, we explore a world which directly questions the meaning of education itself. There's something extraordinary about asking an 8-year-old to stay onstage for a 90 minute story. Asha was amazing, and was joined by Farah (they shared the role). Experts visited us, such as Prof Genevieve von Petzinger, who gave us insight into geometric symbols in the Upper Palaeolithic cave systems. The sound world developed, meaning that the show could be experienced entirely through headphones. When *Deciphering* finally opened, the +25-year-old Elise abseiled through the ceiling of our classroom, the floor did (in the end) rise and fall to reveal a cave. The final monologue and gesture of the play, authored by Craig Hamilton, captured the essence of our story. To be brave. You can't fail if you're brave, it's literally not possible.

October 2025

Time has passed since we first created the show. The story, however, remains as a rich part of the cultural heritage of **curious directive**, and associated artists. We are gathering again to revisit the story for schools across the UK.

Jack Lowe

The ticket/information office at Font-de-Gaume in The Lot, France - 2017

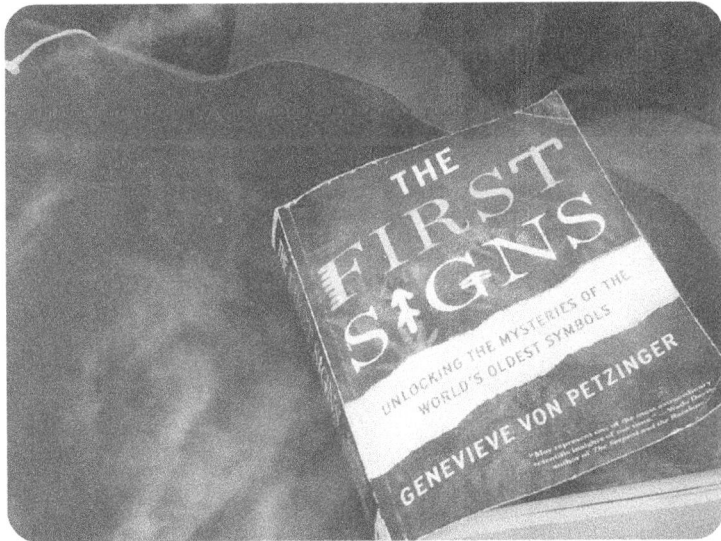

Genevieve von Petzinger's 'The First Signs' on the dashboard of a hire car whilst visiting The Lot, Dordogne, France - 2017

The team for the early workshops, Norwich - 2020

Mother (Steph Street) and Daughter (Asha Sylvestre) trace symbols in the workshop - 2020

Headphones, post-it notes and imagery as the design arrives, Norwich - 2021

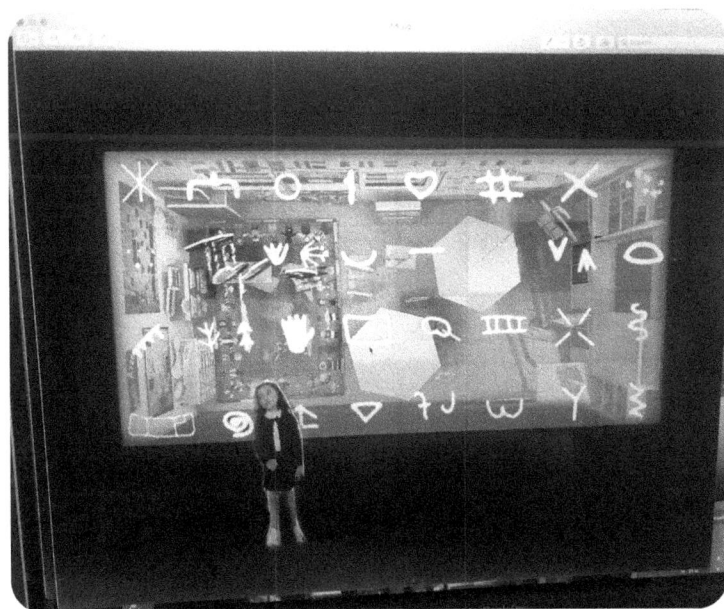

Early design concept from Zoë Hurwitz and Jack Lowe, Norwich - 2021

'Bombo' carry out field recordings - Sulawesi, Indonesia, 2021

Bombo and Jack Lowe capture drone footage for the 'basecamp' of the Deciphering story - Sulawesi, Indonesia, 2021

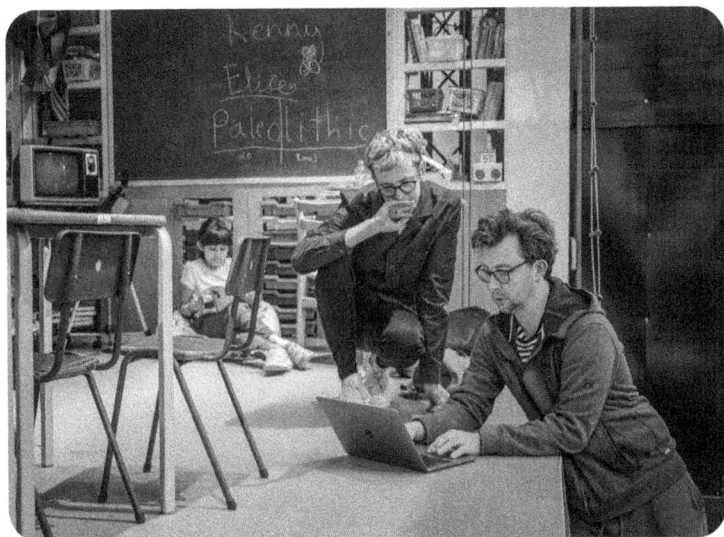

Lewis Mackinnon and Jack Lowe work through some script, as Asha Sylvestre takes in the props. - Norwich, 2021

Amanda Hadingue, Jack Lowe, Faizal Abdullah and Steph Street work through scenes on the rehearsal set. - Norwich, 2021

Sarita Gabony and Jade Hunter watch rehearsals.
- Norwich, 2021

Rehearsing on set with full company.
- Norwich, 2021

Ardi (Faizal Abdullah) and Juliette (Sarita Gabony) at the bottom of the cave - New Diorama Theatre, 2021 - (c) Alex Brenner.

Elise (Farah Qadir) and Kenny (Lewis Mackinnon) in the classroom - New Diorama theatre, 2021 - (c) Alex Brenner.

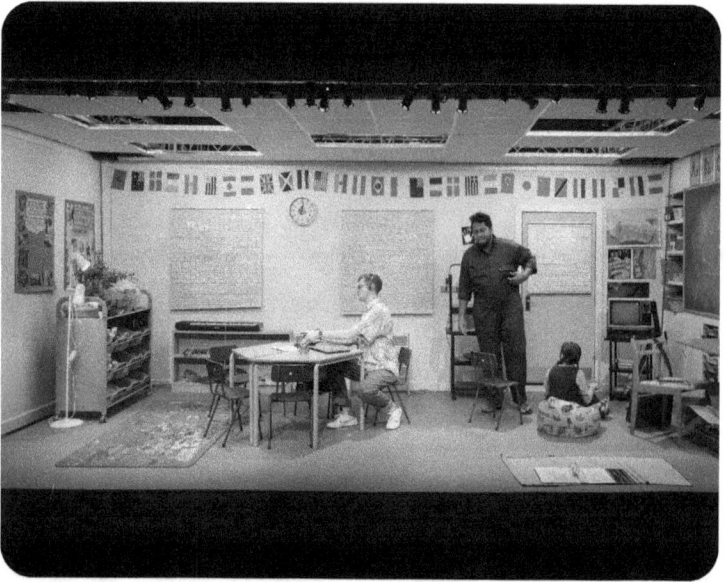

Kenny (Lewis Mackinnon), Reza (Faizal Abdullah) and Elise (Asha Sylvestre) - New Diorama Theatre, 2021 - (c) Alex Brenner.

Elise (Farah Qadir) and Kenny (Lewis Mackinnon) in the classroom - New Diorama theatre, 2021 - (c) Alex Brenner.

DECIPHERING *is a curious directive and New Diorama Theatre co-production.* devised by curious directive, **conceived by Jack Lowe.**

ORIGINAL CAST

Elise, at 8 years old	Asha Sylvestre & Farah Qadir
Elise, at 25 years old / Juliette	Sarita Gabony
Elise, at 48 years old	Stephanie Street
Kenny Robbins	Lewis Mackinnon
Marie-Claude Gichard / Mrs Peters	Amanda Hadingue
Ardi / Reza / Indra Bin-Johan	Faizal Abdullah

CREATIVES

Direction	Jack Lowe
Design	Zoë Hurwitz
Light	Katherine Graham
Sound	Kieran Lucas / Pete Malkin
Field Sound	Bombo
Composition	Theo Whitworth
Video editing	Jack Lowe
Deputy Stage Manager	Chloe Forestier-Walker
Technical Stage Manager	Tom Clutterbuck
3D modelling	Jordan Albon
Production Manager	Rhys Thomas
Touring Production Manager	James Boyer-Smith
Paleoanthropologist	Prof. Genevieve von Petzinger
Graphic Design	Jasmine Robinson
Rehearsal Photography	James Boyer-Smith
Additional Photography	Katherine Mager
Production Photography	Alex Brenner

ADDITIONAL CREATIVES / TECHNICAL CONTRIBUTIONS

Craig Hamilton, Jade Hunter, Jennifer Jackson, Suzie Kirk-Dumitru, Norah Lopez-Holden, Katherine Newman, Patrick Osborne, Natalie Songer, Sophie Steer & Sachin Sylvestre.

CURIOUS DIRECTIVE (2025)

Artistic Director / CEO	Jack Lowe
Producer	Molly Farley

www.curiousdirective.com

Deciphering

Characters

FRANCE

Juliette, *an ophthalmologist, mother of* **Elise**
Ardi, *a struggling filmmaker, father of* **Elise**

JAKARTA, INDONESIA (the school)

Mrs Peters, *head teacher, Jakarta International School*
Reza, *janitor, Jakarta International School*
Kenny *Robbins, new primary school teacher, Jakarta International School*

SULAWESI, INDONESIA (the cave)

Indra *Bin Johan, palaeoarchaeologist (site manager)*
Marie-Claude *Gichard, palaeoarchaeologist (pigment specialist)*

Elise *is played by three separate actors, at different ages in her life:*
Elise, *aged eight at Jakarta International School*
Elise, *aged twenty-five at Oxford University studying a PhD in Palaeo-archaeology*
Elise, *aged forty-eight, a graphic designer*

In the text, the use of a forward slash (/) denotes an active silence.

Deciphering *is set across three main locations. Firstly, the primary school. The action in the primary school is set over one day in the mid-1980s. These scenes play out as one continuous gesture underneath and over the top of the other locations/scenes. It's like one durational scene which drifts in and out of focus. The stage space should accommodate this staging to best achieve the cross-references in time/space from* **Elise'**s *life.*

The second location is set in/around a newly discovered cave system in Southern Sulawesi (also Indonesia). This is a real-life cave system which inspired the show **Deciphering***. Collaborators on the creation of the project, an audio-visual duo called Bombo, were given world-first access to a site with cave paintings and symbols from 40,000 years ago. Characters are fictionalised but are based on their experiences at the real-life site.*

The final location for the story follows alternative lives for the character of **Elise** *(aged twenty-five). These should be staged with a child-like sensibility, as if stretching forward in time from the perspective of a child, rather than retrospectively from the perspective of an adult.*

Deciphering *is dedicated to Ken Robinson, maverick schools educator, who also inspired the show.*

Deciphering *started after the director, Jack Lowe, visited one of the few remaining polychromatic painted cave sites open to the public. He was shown a child's handprint, impossibly suspended six feet in the air.*

Pre-setting

The audience take their seats and put on a pair of comfortable, wired-in headphones. The entire story is experienced through headphones, like a museum exhibit. However, the headphones almost dissolve into the story after the first scene. You forget you are wearing them.

On putting them on, as an audience member, you hear distant thunder and light rain on a tin roof.

1985, Jakarta (Indonesia). *It's dawn. We see a dimly lit portacabin primary school classroom with a tropical storm passing over.*

Through two square windows we see a playground, poised, ready for the arrival of young people. There is one main door into the classroom and a 'fire escape' style door.

We hear a gentle dawn chorus birdsong sheltering from the storm. The birdsong is particular to Jakarta.

The light from outside is muted, but sharp.

The classroom contains six interlocked, hexagonal tables. Small blue chairs are tucked under, suitable for eight-year-olds. Empty cans on the tables contain felt-tips and crayons. There's a music corner, a discovery corner and a blackboard. There's an overhead projector with acetate and a fan on the wall.

There are some red textbooks. Across the back wall are flags of the world. On the floor is a rug, with a map of the world. The ceiling is made from tiles, but, curiously, there are five missing, leaving holes in the ceiling.

There's a corner for a teacher, but the contents of the desk have been cleared.

Below the portacabin, there is a dark abyss.

Above the portacabin, there is evidence of climbing equipment, ropes and pullies.

The sound builds.

Scene One

9 months before Elise I

A polychromatic cave, the Dordogne, France, 1977.

We see the action take place in the dark abyss described in front of the classroom.

The text '9 months before Elise' appears across the back wall in hand-drawn letters. A home video of **Juliette** *begins, showing her with* **Ardi**.

We hear distinct sounds of an ancient cave system. Gradually, their exchanges come into focus.

Juliette, *in full caving gear, is struggling to adjust her harness. She's French, but fluent in English.* **Ardi** *is also in full caving gear. He is Indonesian and speaks broken English. A gentle lull of a strange nursery rhyme plays in the distance of the sound design.*

We hear **Juliette** *first.*

Juliette   Ardi?

Ardi   Hello!

He calls into the depths of the cave.

Juliette   Where are you?

Ardi *calls into the depths of the cave again.*

Ardi   Hello!

Juliette   ARDI! Stop. Where are you? Come back.

Ardi   I'm here, Juliette. I'm here.

Juliette *is hovering five metres above* **Ardi**.

Juliette   Ok I'm going to put the rope down –

Ardi   – Remember what we talked about. Be careful –

Juliette   – Alright out the way. Ok. Coming down.

Ardi *has a Super 8 camera. As she descends, he commentates, awkwardly channelling David Attenborough's pitch and tone.*

Ardi   Look down.

Juliette   Stop it! Hello!

She sees him. Blows a kiss. She descends.

OK I'm going to do the tricky part.

She pushes herself off the bottom of the classroom and descends towards the floor.

Ardi   'As she descends into the cave, this beautiful French heroine Juliette reveals her beauty.'

She reaches the bottom

Juliette   Alight

Ardi *turns to inspect the stalagmites and stalactites.*

Ardi   Isn't this amazing?

Juliette   Oof. I'm hot. Ok. Where are we going?

Ardi   Ok watch your step.

He turns and they both make their way under the classroom and into the depths of the cave.

The ropes disappear up.

Scene Two

+8 years – Kenny is introduced to the classroom

1985, Jakarta.

We're in the classroom from the pre-set. In contrast to the cave, it's bright and hot, whilst maintaining an early morning feeling.

As the sound builds out of the cave, the text '+ 8 years' is scrawled across the classroom wall.

Mrs Peters *interrupts the action by switching on the light.*

Mrs Peters *is the head teacher, officious and strict.* **Kenny** *is a new teacher, with a leather satchel and far too warmly dressed for this time and place.*

Entering –

Mrs Peters   Good trip?

Kenny   Yes, thank you. Well, a little bit jet-lagged –

Mrs Peters   – Oh well the heat in Jakarta at this time of year won't help that I'm afraid. There is a water cooler in the corridor. Fan's broken at the moment, but at least it's a mostly empty classroom today, so –

The top lights flicker on and off rapidly, interrupting her.

– Ah yes, the power has a few shortages, so just hold tight annnnnnd –

The lights come back on.

– ah there we are. Yes, so the children are on a field trip today, to look at some caves with Mr Cliff.

Kenny   Mr Cliff?

Mrs Peters   Yes. It's an all-day thing so you'll have a chance to settle in. Right, well what have we got for you. So, an OHP, television and video player . . . really anything should need for a good start to their education.

Kenny   Ok. Great thank you.

Mrs Peters   Ah, yes. Lesson plans are over there in the corner. Please familiarise yourself with those. We offer a broad range here. Science, History. Some arts and humanities but we try to keep things aligned with, well with learning which will lead to successful careers.

Kenny   Right, ok.

Mrs Peters   I need to pop back to the office now. But if you need anything, do just ask Reza.

Kenny   Reza.

Mrs Peters   Yes. He'll sort you out.

Kenny   Thank you, Mrs Peters.

Mrs Peters *exits in a flourish.* **Kenny** *puts his coat on the teacher's chair. He takes out a Rubik's Cube and places it on his desk. He explores the room, muttering to himself. He finds the electric keyboard in the music corner. He accidently plays an automated jingle.*

Reza *knocks.*

Kenny   Hello?

Reza *enters. A huge, friendly man, in a boiler suit.*

Reza   Good morning!

Reza *and* **Kenny** *shake hands and interact.*

Kenny   Reza. I'm Mr Robbins. Kenny.

Reza   KENNY! Like Kenny Rogers.

Kenny   Yeah.

Reza   I come to fix the OHP.

Kenny   Thank you, Reza.

Reza *settles into his work.*

Reza   Mr Kenny. Where you come from?

Kenny   Scotland.

Reza   Scotland! Kenny Dalglish! Liverpool. 'You'll never walk –'

Kenny *doesn't know the song.*

Kenny   – I don't know.

Reza '. . . alone!' You don't know Liverpool FC?

Kenny No, sorry.

Reza *continues his work fixing the OHP.*

Reza Mr Kenny. First time in Jakarta.

Kenny The heat is quite something.

Reza Ah, yes. Jakarta very hot. Very busy. Not like Scotland.

Kenny Definitely not.

Reza Beautiful country. Scotland.

Kenny Beautifu–

Reza – Many castles.

Kenny Yes, beautiful history.

Reza Ah yes. History. Glasgow Rangers. Celtic. Kilmarnock. Aberdeen.

Kenny Yep.

Reza Mr Kenny, OHP fixed.

Kenny Great. Thank you, Reza.

Reza No problem. If you need anything. You come and find Reza. Good luck!

Kenny *writes his name on the blackboard. Underlines it heavily.*

Elise, *an eight-year-old girl, walks in. She has a raincoat on and a school bag. She hangs up her coat.*

She turns to look at **Kenny**.

Kenny Hello.

Elise Hi.

/

Kenny What's your name?

Elise   Elise

Kenny   Nice to meet you, Elise. My name is Mr Robbins.

They stare at each other. Nothing happens. Eventually, **Kenny** *takes the lead.*

Kenny   Would you . . . would you like to write your name on the board in chalk?

Elise *writes her name on the board. Draws a heart from the end of the 'e' of her name.*

Kenny   Eliiissee. That's lovely. All joined up. With a squiggle.

He quickly rubs his name off the board and writes 'Kenny'. And copies the squiggle.

Kenny   I think you can call me Kenny, as that's my name.

Elise   Hi, Kenny.

/

Kenny   Er. Shall we start with some music?

Elise   Ok.

Kenny   Do you play any instruments?

Elise   I can play the keyboard.

Kenny   Really? Cool. I'd love to hear it.

She plays 'Twinkle, Twinkle, Little Star'. **Kenny** *encourages.*

Kenny   What? That's amazing! But what are you doing playing to the wall? You should be on a world tour.

He sets up a stadium crowd.

I'm imagining front-row seats. I'm imagining a single spotlight and the crowd going wild . . . for ELISE!

He beckons her to play again. She plays a full rendition of 'Twinkle, Twinkle, Little Star'.

Kenny   Woah. Jazzy. I love that. that was so cool. I can't play any instruments.

He spots a tongue drum on the table.

Listen, do you know what that is?

He's pointing to a tongue drum.

Elise   Yeah, it's a tongue drum.

Kenny   A tongue drum. Can you play it?

Elise   No, not really.

Kenny   Give it a go.

She does. He watches.

Kenny   I've got an idea. Why don't we write some music together?

Have you ever written any music before?

Do you know how to write some musical symbols.

Do you know what this is?

Elise   A treble clef?

*The lights fade on **Kenny** and **Elise**. They stay in the classroom for the remainder of the story.*

Care should be taken to clearly map out the inner life of their character arc.

However, it is likely their activities, whilst happening in real time, will need to accommodate other scenes taking place on top of them – so should not pull too much focus.

Scene Three

+48 years – The cave I

*2025, London. Small flat of **Elise**, aged forty-eight. As the sound builds out of the cave, the text '+ 48 years' is scrawled across the classroom wall.*

Elise *is talking to a colleague in French.*

Elise   *Allez, regardons ensemble.* [Ok let's look together.]

Attend, c'est juste en train de télécharger. [Wait, it's just downloading.]

Si si, c'est pour la semaine prochaine, il n'y a pas souci. [Yes it's for next week, don't worry.]

Donc, je vois le petit coeur avec la spirale à l'interier. Oui, c'est pas mal. [Ok, I see the little heart with the spiral in the interior. Yes, not bad.]

Et si on la déplace pour avoir la spirale qui enchaine du coeur . . . qu'est que t'en pense? [And if you put the spiral following the heart, what do you think?]

Tu vois? Moi, je réfléchi. [You see? Now I'm re-thinking it.]

Je fais pas n'importe quoi après plusieurs verres de vins . . . [I don't do anything stupid after several glasses of wine.]

Another call comes in.

Attend, Pascale – il y a quelqu'un qui m'appelle. [Hang on, Pascale. Someone's calling me.]

Restez-là. Ne raccroche pas. [Stay there. Don't hang up.]

Elise *picks up. It's* **Marie-Claude**, *her PhD supervisor from many years ago.*

Elise   Hello?

Marie-Claude   Hello, Elise?

Elise   *Oui.*

Marie-Claude   C'est Marie-Claude. Marie-Claude Gichard. *Ca va?* [It's Marie-Claude. Marie-Claude Gichard. How are you?]

Elise   *Ca va, et toi?*

Marie-Claude   *Ca va.* Is this a bad time to talk?

Elise   Er, no. No.

Marie-Claude   I wondered if you received my email?

Elise   Er, yes, yes I did.

Marie-Claude   Ok. You know I am not at Oxford anymore. I'm in Paris now, at the Musée d'Archaeologie –

Elise   Ok.

Marie-Claude   Did you look at the photo of the cave in Indonesia?

Elise   I did, yes –

Marie-Claude   – Then perhaps you know what I'm going to ask you?

Elise   – No. No I don't.

Marie-Claude   I have been contacted by a colleague of mine. Indra Bin Johan. You know his work?

Elise   Yes. He's working with uranium series dating. I've read about him.

Marie-Claude   Yes, he's in Sulawesi at the moment, managing this cave. He's working with Griffith University, and he's asked me if I'll go over there and give my opinion. Elise – the symbols you can see in this photo – that is just one of the panels in the cave.

/

Elise   Oh.

Marie-Claude   Yes. Listen my expertise is with pigment and so –

Elise   – Marie-Claude –

Marie-Claude   – Please don't hang up, Elise, please just talk –

Elise   – Marie-Claude, I appreciate you getting in touch and, for sending me this astonishing image. Truly. But I can't. My life has moved on. I moved on a long time ago –

Marie-Claude   – Elise exactly! Exactly. You're not my student anymore. It is the past. Right now. This site. These symbols. I think the symbols are really important. And your interpretation of what they could be, could be really, really helpful to Indra, the history of this place, and –

Elise   – and to you?

Marie-Claude   Yes. And to me. I can take someone with me, and I want it to be you.

/

Hello?

/

Elise *begins joining* **Marie-Claude** *in the same part of the stage.*

Elise   Ok. Ok. Yes.

Marie-Claude *leaves,* **Elise** *follows.*

Scene Four

+8 years – The history lesson

Kenny *is muttering to himself as* **Elise** *finishes writing her music. He walks over to the desk and looks at the lesson plan. He comes straight in with:*

Kenny (*muttering to himself*)   Let's see. Water cycle. Food chain. Geography. Oh, deep history.

(*On finding acetate folder.*) Elise. Do you know how this works, Elise?

Do we take it out from the wall?

Elise   You just have to press this black switch at the back.

She turns it on with ease.

Kenny   Ah. We have light.

He turns off the main light on the wall. He takes a piece of acetate with a woolly mammoth on it.

Let's see. What have we got here? You know what these are, right?

Elise   Er . . . woolly mammoths, I think?

Kenny   That's right! Woolly mammoths. And they roamed the earth during the last ice age. Or the Upper Palaeolithic Period. Do you know what 'palaeolithic' means?

Elise   No.

Kenny *goes to the blackboard and writes 'Palaeolithic' on the board.*

Kenny   Do you know what 'palaeo' means? Have a guess?

Elise   Pale?

Kenny   Good guess. But it means old. Do you want to write 'palaeo' on the board?

Elise   Ok.

Kenny   So, 'palaeo' means old. And 'lithic' means rocks, or stones. So, we can call it the Palaeolithic Period, or we can call it the Old Stone Age. And during this time, the Earth, it was really cold. So – early humans, they lived in caves to keep warm –

Elise   – Cool.

Kenny *changes the acetate to a slide of Lascaux in France (cave paintings).*

Kenny   Just like this one. See here, what can you see?

Elise   Cows and horses. And reindeer.

Kenny   That's right – we now call those cows bison. And yeah, there are horses, just like today and reindeer too.

Elise   One, two, three, four.

Kenny   And this was discovered in 1940. Lascaux.

He puts a third acetate onto the OHP, of a handprint.

And this one, I think you'll like. Can you tell me what it is?

Elise   A handprint. Woah.

Kenny   Yeah. It's a negative handprint. Made using pigment on a wall. What do you think they were trying to say? To us now?

Elise   Hello?

Kenny   Hello from history.

They look at the image together.

I've got an idea. I want us to imagine history in a timeline. I want you to write down your date of birth on here. Ok? What's your date of birth.

Elise   21 January 1977.

Kenny   Now I want you to write today's date?

Elise   1985.

Kenny   So, you're eight.

Elise   Yeah.

Kenny   Great. So, what we're going to do is go forwards in time from the Palaeolithic over here all the way to 1985. 40,000 . . . 30,000 . . . 20,000 . . . Christ! . . . CE 500 . . . CE 1500 . . . 1977 (your actual birthday) and 1985 (today of all days).

They do this together across the classroom. **Elise** *watches* **Kenny** *for a moment, realising he is definitely not like the other teachers in the school.*

Kenny   And on the vertical axis, we could use this to think about your future, which is unwritten, unknown.

Elise   Yeah.

Kenny   So where might Elise be in ten years' time?

Elise   I'll be eighteen. Maybe I'll go to university.

Kenny   Oh, fancy.

Elise   Fancy schmanzy.

Kenny   Where might ELISE be when she's twenty-five?

Elise   I don't know.

Kenny   What sort of interests might you have? Where in the world might you live? Maybe you could be an ice skater?

Elise   Could do.

Kenny   You want to pop that up on our timeline?

Elise   You could be a rock star? You could be an explorer?

The lights fade on **Kenny** *and* **Elise***.*

Scene Five

+25 years – Elise in a PhD supervision, Oxford University – 2002

Elise*, aged twenty-five, descends through the ceiling of the portacabin in a harness.*

She disconnects her harness.

Marie-Claude *enters, with academic papers in her hand.*

Kenny *and* **Elise** *move to the TV corner in the classroom.*

Elise *and* **Marie-Claude** *both sit at the children's-size table and chairs.*

A symbol of the lineage between a primary school setting and university – part of the same continuum.

Marie-Claude   Elise, it's so good to meet you in person, finally.

Elise   Thank you. You too.

/

Marie-Claude   Well, your idea is, uh, provocative.

Elise   – Yes, thank you.

Marie-Claude   So you're fresh from an MA on geometric symbols?

Elise   Yes –

Marie-Claude   Ok so I have your doctoral proposal in full here. So let me see: 'A non-Euro centric approach to the deciphering of abstract geometric symbols in Ice Age cave art.' Quite a mouthful this one.

Elise   Yes.

Marie-Claude   Ok, so why the symbols, and not the art?

Elise   Well. Because whilst the cave art, the bison, are interesting, I think these signs, these geometric shapes . . . they show that Ice Age people had *already* developed a form of thinking that we may be able to regard as a precursor to language, to writing –

Marie-Claude   – Wow. Well, that is huge for a PhD –

Elise   I believe they were using a limited number of symbols. And if there are only thirty-two signs, barring a few outliers, used from 40,000 to 10,000 years ago, then surely these markings are trying to transmit some kind of information.

Marie-Claude   Ok. Ok. And talk to me about the other aspect of your thesis, what is this about 'non-Eurocentric'? I don't follow this.

Elise   Why are we just looking at Europe? There must be more. I mean I could go to Australia, South Asia, I'd like to go back to Indonesia, where I went to school. Wherever people were making geometric marks in caves. Not just in France.

Marie-Claude   Yeah. But, Elise, France is the epicentre of Ice Age art. Are you wanting to disrupt this? You've been in France this summer?

Elise   And Spain, yes. I've the beginnings of a database in Europe. But there must be more.

Marie-Claude   I mean that is great. But that trip needs to be sort of a working holiday really. Because, you need to be developing a whole methodology from a robust literature review. There's an order to these things, really.

/

Marie-Claude *senses* **Elise** *is disappointed about being slowed down with her thinking.*

Marie-Claude   And I notice you want to include linguistics in this too?

Elise   Oh. I think so.

Marie-Claude   Well, I think you must be careful because mixing departments can be uncomfortable. It is tricky. You try to jump between departments, it's like trying to square the circle. Also. Well, I want you here in Archaeology.

Elise   It's an interdisciplinary pursuit.

Marie-Claude   Yah, this is unusual.

Scene Six

+48 years – The invitation

Sulawesi (Indonesia).

Marie-Claude, **Elise** *and* **Indra** *are sat in an off-road truck. The driver (unseen) negotiates a pothole filled road. It is hot, dusty and noisy.*

Marie-Claude *is asleep.*

Elise *is looking out the window of the truck.*

Indra *is lighting a cigarette, and the scene comes straight in with –*

Elise   Indra. When was the cave first discovered here?

Indra   Oh, quite recently. We had a 5.5 tremor, and a small landslide tore away a tree – revealed the cave. Problem is, water from the paddy field floods straight into the cave. I got Marie-Claude onto the list as soon as I could. You're a symbols expert, right?

Elise   Used to be.

/

Can I get one of those?

Indra   Sure.

Elise   I love the smell.

They smoke. Taking in the landscape.

Elise   I read your article in *Nat Geo*. Incredible.

Indra   I love fieldwork. The rush of it, you know? Been on the site for a month already. But it has its drawbacks. I miss my little boy. Here I show you, his picture.

Elise   What's his name?

Indra   Raihan. Eight years old. Loves digging. Which uni are you at?

Elise   Oh, well, I'm not researching anymore.

Indra *speaks, throughout the story, to fellow colleagues and support staff in Indonesian.*

Indra   *Bima! Ayuh cepet dong. Nanti kita bisa telat tau . . .* [Bima! Go quicker please, or else we'll be late.]

Marie-Claude *wakes with a start.*

Marie-Claude   How long was I out?

Elise *passes her water.*

Indra   About an hour. Jet lag catching up.

Marie-Claude   Are we near?

Indra   Yeah about 15 minutes from drop-off point. The rains were very bad this morning, so going will be slow.

They immediately stand and take trek positions as if halfway through the trek.

Elise   Can we slow down?

Indra   Ok, take on some water.

Marie-Claude   Indra, this is all just farmland across there?

Indra   This is paddy field, rice, it'll gradually drop off as we get further into the jungle area, through the trees, there's no real owner, technically the central Indonesian government I guess, if anyone asked.

But you can see that limestone cliffs rise up, seemingly from nowhere. beautiful right?

Marie-Claude   Yes, and are there also caves inside the cliffs?

Indra   Definitely. UNESCO are already very excited. Our site is about 8 kilometres over this direction. Out of view. We need to get across a river, and then the rock gap is a little further on.

Elise   What's the rock gap?

Indra   Oh, it's an opening in the limestone cliffs, just as wide as one person. It's the only way in and out of the village.

Marie-Claude, **Elise** *and* **Indra** *step into the base-camp hut. It's created using a simple roll of bamboo matting on the floor, within the classroom.*

Indra *confirms something with the team outside.*

Indra   *Rano, Pak Muin ke mana?* [Rano, where did Pak Muin go?]

Kok gak ada yang ngasih tau . . . [No one told me.]

Tamu dari Perancis udah tiba loh. [The guests from France are here.]

Dia pulang pagi esok? Ok gitu, yaudah. Rano, makan malam sudah siap? Makasih! [It's alright. When is he back, tomorrow? Alright, thanks. Rano, please prepare the dinner.]

Elise   I'm gutted we can't get down there, to see it today.

Marie-Claude   So, this is our home for the next four days. I hope you like chickens.

Indra *moves to the table with his laptop.*

Indra   Ok, guys. Pak Muin is away today. He's the one in charge, the guardian of the cave. But he's back tomorrow morning. But. Come take a look. I have a 3D scan of the cave.

Marie-Claude/Elise *join* **Indra** *by the table.*

Indra   So if you hover in. From the mouth of the cave to the drop of the chamber is about 150 metres and then . . . magic.

Marie-Claude   Oh, it's fantastic. But scroll back a little. Yeh there. There are no walkways in place.

Indra   Nope.

Marie-Claude   No temperature control? On the walls it's very wet and the floor.

Elise   What's that showing up there?

Indra   This is all algae. So when you go in, we'll take it slow. There is a wire ladder to help us descend down into the chamber.

He calls back outside.

Ya? Makasih! Kita datang nih! [Yes? Thanks! We're coming.]
Ok come, food is ok outside. MC, you're ok with fish/rice?

Indra *and* **Marie-Claude** *leave.*

Elise *takes a minute.*

Elise+48 *sees* **Elise+8**, *for the first time, who comes over to look into the laptop. It's shocking for* **Elise+48** *to be looking at data which might well back up her theories from years ago. After a moment,* **Marie-Claude** *comes back in.*

Marie-Claude   Elise?

Elise   Sorry.

She leaves.

Scene Seven

9 months before Elise II

A polychromatic cave, the Dordogne, France, 1977.

The text '9 months before Elise' appears across the back wall in hand-drawn letters. A video of **Juliette** *begins, showing her with* **Ardi**.

Juliette *appears from under the classroom. This time she has the Super 8 camera.*

Juliette   You alright behind, Ardi?

Ardi   Yes, I can see you.

Juliette   Ok. Watch your head.

Ardi   You hear the water dripping from above.

Juliette   Of course. Makes me want to wee.

Ardi   Did I turn off the kitchen tap?

Juliette   Ardi. I don't know.

Ardi   Shit.

Juliette   Forget about it. Down here.

Ardi   Yah.

They move through the cave.

So . . . have you . . . have you thought about it some more?

Juliette   About what?

Ardi   About trying. Trying for a little one.

Juliette   Oh. Ardi. No, not really yet.

Ardi   Ok. Well, when you're ready. We've got to go through here.

They again disappear underneath the classroom.

Scene Eight

+8 years – The art lesson

Elise *and* **Kenny** *are in different parts of the classroom.* **Kenny** *is looking through the minimal art supplies.* **Elise** *is sat on a beanbag, reading a book.*

Kenny *turns to* **Elise**.

Kenny   Elise? What are you reading?

Elise *is reading a book on beanbags.*

Elise   A book about prehistoric animals.

Kenny *looks at the limited art supplies.*

Kenny   Shall we do some art? Maybe we could draw these animals? What would you like to use. Pencils? Chalk?

Elise   Can we use the paints?

Kenny   We can, yeah. Let's put on these overalls. Stand on Australia.

He's referring to the carpet map of the world.

What are you going to draw? Something from your book on prehistoric animals?

Elise   An Arctic wolf.

Kenny   What's the difference between an Arctic wolf and a normal wolf?

Elise   I think they live in different habitats.

Kenny   I think you might be right.

They get the spray paints out.

Kenny *goes to get paper from a drawer. They start spraying.*
Kenny *sees the Picasso line drawings on the wall.*

Kenny   I see you've been studying Picasso. You know he spent his whole life trying to draw like a child. So, you were already born an artist.

Mrs Peters *comes in with a jug of juice.*

Mrs Peters   Oh. Elise, there you are. I thought you were in my office. Waiting.

Kenny   We are –

Mrs Peters   – using the cannister paints. I see.

Kenny   She's very creative.

Mrs Peters   And what are we spraying?

Elise   An Arctic wolf.

Mrs Peters   Oh lovely. And this is in the context of broader Art History, is it?

Kenny   Well. We were talking about the palaeolithic and Picasso.

Mrs Peters   So, is it History or is it Art?

Kenny   It's both.

Mrs Peters   Is it? That's interesting. Well, I'm very glad you're getting on. That's lovely. Just make sure you have a lunch break.

Kenny   What time is lunch?

Mrs Peters   Reza will bring you something around 12:15 p.m.

Mrs Peters *beckons* **Kenny** *over to the other side of the classroom.*

Mrs Peters   Mr Robbins, if you wouldn't mind refraining from using cannister paints indoors in the future please.

She exists, abruptly, slamming the door.

Kenny   Hey, Elise, why don't we try 'mixed media'. Maybe some chalks. Red, yellow, both?

Elise   Both!

Kenny   Maybe we could pretend we're at a gallery opening. Lots of free wine. Madam?

Elise   Mr.

They both drink some of the warm juice.

Kenny   Mmmm. Warm.

I love using spray paints. You know when you're older, you could be an artist using spray paints?

*They start putting the pictures up on **Elise***'s timeline.*

Scene Nine

+25 years – Elise as a graffiti artist – 2002

A city in Europe.

Elise *descends into the classroom space through the ceiling in a harness.*

She's singing to herself with headphones on.

She sprays a symbol, using her hand as a stencil on the door. Her phone rings.

Elise   Hello, Papa.

Ardi   Elise, you're awake!

Elise   Yeah –

Ardi   – I was planning to leave you a message.

Elise   No, I'm still up.

Ardi   It's morning here. Just got my feet up looking out at the city.

Elise   I miss home.

Ardi   Just calling to say . . . hello.

Elise   Hi, Dad . . .

Ardi   Me and your mother were just clearing your room. We found my old Super 8.

Elise   Oh yeah, sorry I must have kept it in there. I love watching your old videos of Mum.

Ardi   What videos?

Elise   The ones of you on holiday?

Ardi   Oh, right, yes, that's fine. I found an old painting you made when you were eight. It's some sort of dog. We've put it back on the fridge.

Elise   That's cute, Dad. Shall I call you tomorrow.

Ardi   Alright. Just call me when you're free. Elise. Be careful.

Elise *breaks the fourth wall.*

Elise   What do you want to be when you grow up? Growing up, I watched my dad work with his video camera. A hobby. He never pursued filmmaking. Or an artistic life. He told me I should. Try to forge a new path for myself. Away from him, and Mum. So, in this version of myself I'm not at Oxford studying Palaeoarchaeology. In this version of myself I'm twenty-five and I'm at art school trying to follow my dad's forgotten dreams. I've been looking for the most difficult spot to get to. I've made my mark.

I was here.

Scene Ten

+48 years – The invitation

Sulawesi (Indonesia). **Indra**, **Elise** *and* **Marie-Claude** *are on the short trek to the mouth of the cave. They have dry bags, hard hats and head torches. They pause, standing over the edge of the classroom, looking down into the abyss.*

They turn on their radios together. The sound from now on is 'tinny', as if heard from a radio.

Indra   Shall we go back a few thousand years?

They begin to move through the cave. The music soars. In the original production, the floor of the classroom began to the rise (on a hydraulic lift), creating an even larger gap between the classroom and the floor.

A metal rope ladder can be seen.

They all stop and look over the edge again.

Indra   The water is about 5 centimetres deep, you'll feel it around your feet. You see over there it's coming from there, a small stream from the paddy fields.

Marie-Claude   Ok. Elise. Shall I go first?

Elise   Yes please.

Marie-Claude   Ok.

The effort of climbing down into the cave is heard.

Marie-Claude   Ok I'm at the bottom.

Indra Elise. Down you go.

/

Marie-Claude Oh my God. They are everywhere.

/

Elise Ok. I'm clear.

/

Marie-Claude Elise. It's so much more beautiful than the photos, than the scan.

Elise *gets to the bottom and turns. Loses her breath. There is a moment between* **Marie-Claude** *and* **Elise** *as* **Indra** *descends.*

Marie-Claude *then moves to look across all three of the panels in the cave chamber. Her interaction with* **Indra** *drifts sonically into the background. Her spoken text becomes an underscore to* **Elise's** *lines, 'Hello. How did you get here?' etc.*

Marie-Claude This is . . . this is extraordinary, Indra. *But listen* will you come down here and show me through this because I can't quite understand how this has been left to be so wet, so much water. Look it's ten to twelve centimetres here. And there is a passage through here too? Where does that lead to?

Marie-Claude *and* **Indra** *make their way into the darkness.*

Elise *is visibly shaken.*

Elise Hello. How did you get here? Un, deux, trois, quatre, cinq, six, sept, huit, neuf, putain – how many of you are there?

What are you trying to tell us?

When did you get here?

The floor moves back into position of the classroom.

The lights gradually fade back up onto the primary school classroom.

Elise *disappears into the darkness.*

Scene Eleven

+8 years – The language lesson

Elise *is sat at the table drawing.* **Kenny** *sits at his desk reading a John Berger book, smiling. He turns to her.*

Kenny   How many of you are there in your class?

Elise   Twenty. Twenty-one including me.

Kenny   Twenty-one. And this is an international school, so you must speak lots of different languages.

I don't speak any languages. Do you speak any other languages?

Elise   Yes, I speak French.

Kenny   Impressive. Maybe you could teach me some French.

Elise   Ok.

Kenny   How do you say glasses in French?

Elise   *Lunettes.*

Kenny   *Lunettes.* Hands.

Elise   Er. *Mains.*

Kenny   *Mains.* What about book?

Elise   *Livre.*

Kenny   *Livre.* Chair?

Elise   *Chaise.*

Kenny   *Chaise.* What about telescope?

Elise   *Telescope.*

Kenny   Oh. That's an easier one, then. Just telescope with a French accent.

There is a knock at the door. **Kenny** *helps* **Reza** *who enters with a light box.*

Kenny   Hello?

Reza   Mr Kenny.

Reza *speaks to* **Elise** *in Bahasa.* **Reza** *is carrying a huge light box.*

Elise   *Selamat pagi,* [good morning] Om Reza.

Reza   *Selamat pagi. Loh, Elise. Tadi kamu dicariin tuh sama Mrs Peters. Nanti aku bilangin dia kalau kamu di sini.* [Ah, Elise. Good morning. Mrs Peters was looking for you earlier. I'll tell her that you're here.] The hospital was throwing this away. My wife is a nurse there. So I take and repair. Maybe you can use in classroom?

Kenny   What is it?

Reza *speaks to* **Elise** *in Bahasa.*

Reza   Elise, apa nama Inggeris nya sih? Bisa ngeluarin cahaya gitu?

Elise *translates.*

Elise   Light box.

Reza   Light box? No, Mr Kenny, this box is very heavy.

Elise   No, Om Reza. *Lampu.*

Reza   Oh, *lampu!* Light box.

Turns on the light box.

Kenny   We've just been talking about languages, Reza. Maybe we could do some tracing. If I was to write 'light' in English. Maybe, Reza, maybe you could write 'light' in Bahasa.

Reza *turns on the light box and writes* 'lampu'. **Kenny** *writes underneath* 'light'.

Kenny   Maybe we could create our own language. How would you create light in your own language?

Elise   You could do a spiral with a line through it.

Reza   I go now.

Kenny   Ok, Reza.

Reza   Mr Kenny. You'll never walk . . .

Kenny   Alone?

Reza   Yah.

He exits, quietly shutting the door, so the lesson can continue.

Kenny *watches as* **Elise** *draws her new alphabet.*

Kenny   How is that you speak French?

Elise   My mum's French.

Kenny   What does she do?

Elise   She's an ophthalmologist.

Kenny   Oh, that sounds cool.

Scene Twelve

+25 years – Elise as an ophthalmologist – 2002

Elise *+25 descends through a different part of the ceiling. The light box is transformed into an ophthalmologist's display screen.* **Elise** *unclips her harness and picks up a call from* **Juliette,** *her mother.*

Elise   *Maman?*

Juliette   Hello, darling – are you ok?

Elise   Yes, I'm just at work.

Juliette   Ok –

Elise   – I've just seen this patient. I'm not quite sure what I'm dealing with here –

Juliette   – Ok, darling, I think you should talk with a different ophthalmologist. You know we discussed me not helping you too much. It makes things complicated –

Elise   – Yeh I know. It's ok. I just wanted to say that the patient might have something we talked about a long time ago.

Juliette   Really?

Elise   Yes. You know Dad has that thing where he sees dots and squiggles when in the dark.

Juliette   Entopic phenomena, yes.

Elise   Well, today a patient I just consulted with has exactly the same thing. The same issues –

Juliette   – Oh right.

Elise   – Only this patient was seeing loads of different shapes. Squares, circles, feathers.

Juliette   That's unusual.

Elise   Yes, I thought so too. Anyway. I just. I just, it reminded me of you and of Dad. And made me want to call you.

Juliette   That's very sweet, darling.

/

Elise *looks at the results again.*

Elise   Ok. Ok. Chat to you tomorrow.

Juliette   Ok. Speak to you then. *Bisous, bisous.*

She turns to someone. It's the audience but it's also all of us thinking about what we wanted to be.

Elise   What do you want to be when you grow up?

She speaks to the audience again.

Growing up, I knew my mum worked with eyes. Not an optician, or an optometrist, but an ophthalmologist. Top of the tree. When I was eight, I just wanted to be her. Literally her. Maybe that's when my future started pointing to this moment. I'm twenty-five. I feel like I'm still trying this on. In this version of myself I'm trying to be an optometrist. But what if I was an explorer or a graffiti artist? How would that feel? I've followed my mum's footprints to the exact step. Why is that? It's like I have this genetic attachment. Predetermined to be like her. But if I follow this path, to try to be more like my mum, where will I end up? When I'm thirty-five perhaps I become an ophthalmologist. At forty-eight perhaps I go back to the profession and try to start my own practice. And on my sixty-third birthday I'll perhaps be driving down a motorway, it's raining, I can't see much and . . . that's it.

Scene Thirteen

+48 years – Deciphering I (back at base camp)

Marie-Claude *is taking off her soaking shoes/socks.* **Indra** *is sat at the base of the door smoking and looking out at the rain.* **Elise** *is very still.*

Elise   Well, that was ju–

Marie-Claude   – I know.

Elise   I mean. My hands.

Marie-Claude   I know. It's like I was a child again, you know?

Elise   I cannot believe we just saw that.

/

Marie-Claude   What are you thinking?

Elise *is holding some of her old PhD field notes. Etchings. Photographs.*

Elise   I'm thinking how old and young I feel at the same time. And to remember everything from years ago, excavate back in time. I think I need a *Rocky* montage.

They hover over **Elise**'s *old field notes.*

Marie-Claude   These are your old notes?

Elise   Oh. Look at them.

Marie-Claude   This is my handwriting.

Elise   Marie-Claude Gichard. *Ca c'est pas bien . . .*

I counted 147 symbols down there. Across three panels. 12 square metres each.

Marie-Claude   This is, what, twent-five to thirty caves' worth of geometric symbols in one place, right?

/

Chauvet has eighteen individual symbols across the walls –

Elise   – Seventeen

Marie-Claude   – Seventeen individual symbols. And here, here there are, how many?

Elise   I counted thirty individuals. Hello, old friends.

They take a deep breath.

Elise *(+8) has walked over and put OHP on; she is joined by* **Elise** *(+25).*

Kenny *hands her the pen and acetate –* **Elise** *(+8 and +25) begin to etch onto the acetate, which is projected onto the wall, an echo of the history lesson, showing when the curiosity for cave paintings began.*

Marie-Claude *is looking at the old notes.*

Elise   My mind is filling up again. Asterisk, aviform, circle, claviform, cordiform. I ordered them alphabetically.

Marie-Claude   All these Latin names.

Elise   I was twenty-five. I wanted them to have gravitas.

/

Indra *has come downstage to crouch over the notes with* **Marie-Claude** *and continues to smoke.*

Marie-Claude   And cross-hatch, cruciform, cupule *(this helps her continue).*

Elise   Yes and – dot, finger fluting, flabelleform, half-circle, line,

/

Marie-Claude   Indra, the other teams. What did they say?

Indra   They said why are there no paintings. Why are there no bison, no horses?

Elise   Panel one.

Over the top –

Elise   negative hand, open angle, oval, pectiform, penniform,

Marie-Claude   It's stupid, Indra, but I want to call my father to tell him about this, right now. He will be like Marie-Claude, it's four in the morning, come and get me out of this stupid home. And then hang up, so –

Elise   – Panel two.

Over the top.

Elise   positive hand, quadrangle, reniform, scalariform, segmented cruciform, serpentiform, spiral, triangle, uniciform, W-sign, Y-sign and zigzag.

Indra (*to* **Marie-Claude**)   Do you know, most teams sat where you are now. Wondering, scratching their heads.

Marie-Claude   It's like they were trying to send a message for us. We cannot remember how to read it.

Indra   The other teams, they didn't know what they were looking at – they didn't think much of it.

Elise   Panel three.

Elise *+48 rejoins* **Marie-Claude**

Elise   Marie-Claude with them all there. All laid across the three panels. I thought . . . I thought . . .

Marie-Claude   What?

Elise   I thought I'd be able to spot a pattern. I thought we'd go down that ladder, we'd turn, and they'd all make sense. Immediately. I thought I would see a pattern.

Indra   Patterns take time to emerge, Elise. Come. Let's eat.

Indra *and* **Marie-Claude** *leave.* **Elise** *+48 follows.*

Scene Fourteen

+8 years – The photography lesson

Kenny   I love those patterns, Elise. They're beautiful.

Elise *+8*   Thank you.

Elsie *+48*   Thank you.

Blackout. **Elise** *+48 exits in the blackout.*

Kenny   Ok, let's stay still and wait for our eyes to adjust.

Lights back on (once **Elise** *+48 has exited).*

Kenny   And we have light. What do you fancy doing next?

Elise *looks over to the desk.*

Elise   What's in that box?

She and **Kenny** *begin to unpack a box containing a photography developing kit.*

Kenny   A great question. Would you like to open it? So –
This is equipment that we can use to make a photograph
when we don't have a camera. Photography literally means
'drawing with light'. We can lay objects onto magic paper
and expose it to light. First, we have to make sure the room
is completely dark – would you close the blinds for me?

I'm going to change this bulb, for a red one.

He changes the bulb. **Elise** *shuts the blinds. They are both in a red
gloom.*

Kenny   So, what object would you most like to capture
forever?

Elise   That's hard.

Kenny   Have a think.

He prepares the dark-room chemicals.

Elise   My hand.

Kenny   Your hand?

Elise   Yeah.

Kenny   Lovely choice. So – if you put your hand on this
paper. We'll shock the paper with light. Count down for me
from three /

Elise   Two, one –

Kenny *flicks light switches on and off.* **Elise** *+25 descends from
the ceiling.*

Through this scene **Elise** *+25 descends. She watches herself, aged
eight.*

Scene Fifteen

+25 years – Dark-room photographer

Elise *really observes.*

Elise   What do you want to be when you grow up?

This is the moment I fell in love with photography.

When Kenny showed me this magic.

He had this incredible way of leading things.

He could see what interested me.

And then, he gave me his camera.

The first photo I took was of my shoes.

We see this.

The second was of Kenny cleaning his glasses.

We see this.

In this version of myself, I'm twenty-five and I'm a photography teacher.

I'm passing on that tiny fragment of curiosity sown by Kenny.

This is where it all began. For this version of myself.

Looking down on **Kenny**. *She unhooks.* **Kenny** *moves across to the table with* **Elise** *+8*

The floor slowly rises.

Scene Sixteen

+48 years – Cave II

Elise *and* **Marie-Claude** *are back in the cave, analysing the three panels of geometric symbols.*

Elise   This one is beautiful. *Penniform.* Looks like a delicate feather. There's another in that corner. Really different. The lines on this are thinner, sharper. It feels. considered. This one is thicker.

Marie-Claude   Do you think that's because this person is just a better artist? Or because they are being created for the first time.

Elise   Different time periods perhaps.

Marie-Claude   And yet the pigment is the same. Very unusual.

Elise   I keep thinking about that and the spacing too.

/

My eyes are darting in different directions over these walls.

Marie-Claude   You think this is . . . a composition.

Elise   I don't know. It could be.

Marie-Claude   It's possible this is someone trying to copy? Copy one from another.

Elise   It's possible. But these are so low down. It would have to be a child copying their mother. It's an immediate imitation.

Marie-Claude   Yah, look, they are stopping. The line breaks. Stopping and checking. What is this? An art school?

Elise   Well.

Marie-Claude   Wow.

Elise   But look here. This looks the least decided. The hand and finger fluting. It's smeared between the two. It feels like a mistake. Like someone was in here, resting from the sun, you know putting ochre around their neck to keep the mosquitoes away and they just slipped – and their red hand pressed on the wall and they were like . . . Oh.

Marie-Claude   Oh.

Elise   Oh. That's, that's . . . weird looking. But kind of nice. And in that moment millions, billions I don't know, of neurons started firing and saying yes, yes that feels great. What that looks like is a piece of me. My hand. I was here.

Marie-Claude Is it possible that this mistake becomes a sign that is used because over here, there it is a number of times. This mistake becomes a part of how they communicate.

Elise I think it's, I think it's even more deliberate.

Marie-Claude *disappears into the cave.* **Indra** *arrives with his head torch, smoking.*

Elise But I like the idea of the humanity of this here. And elsewhere. Simultaneously. Because if not, we're saying people travelled from Europe to here. We're what, 14,000 kilometres from France. I don't think so. I don't think so, Indra.

Marie-Claude?

Indra *holds the space as* **Elise** *and* **Marie-Claude** *exit. The smoke from* **Indra**'s *cigarette fills the air, as he offers up a passage from the Qur'an.*

Indra What are you trying to tell us? *Qul in tukhfū mā fī ṣudūrikum au tubduhu ya'lam-hullāh, wa ya'lamu mā fis-samāwāti wa mā fil-arḍ, wallāhu 'alā kulli syai`ing qadīr.* [Whether you conceal what is in your hearts or reveal it, Allah will know it. He knows what is in the heavens and what is in the earth. Allah is powerful over everything.]

Scene Seventeen

+25 years – Elise in a PhD supervision, Oxford University – 2002

Time has passed, but we are back in the academic seminar room. The environment is stuffy, intense and uncreative.

Marie-Claude So. Er. Listen. I've had meeting with the linguistics department, and they tell me you've already made a very big leap to suggest that this is either a kind of alphabet, or pictographic alphabet, is that what you're saying?

Elise   I don't see how um –

Marie-Claude   I'm just passing on what they've said to me. It seems with these names; you've already ascribed single definitive meanings to these signs.

Elise   I think it's fairly obvious to me that a handprint is a handprint, and we've got images of feathers, here we can see footprints of birds –

Marie-Claude   – Right, I mean for the linguistics department it isn't obvious. I mean of course, I can say, yes you can look at it and say yes, this appears to look like a feather, and then you turn it the other way, it looks like a tree, this way it could be an arrow, or a spear. But they're talking about this in the context of Rebus. And if you –

Elise   – I'm sorry you're just going to have to remind me of Rebus.

Marie-Claude   Elise. This is it. You are with me, but you are also in the linguistics department, you must know what this is . . . I should have seen this coming . . .

Elise   I just think that it's evident that this is a feather.

Marie-Claude   Wait you're using this word evident agai–

Elise   – Well, for example, what about a handprint, that's undeniable?

Marie-Claude   It's undeniably a hand. But you are suggesting . . . what are you suggesting that it will always mean on a cave wall, hand.

Elise   What I'm suggesting that it's some kind of creative, creative, er, form of identification of oneself. I was here. A gesture to the future.

Marie-Claude   In your Master's studies you didn't cover any linguistics?

Elise   No.

Marie-Claude   Well, I'm just wondering if it might be worth enrolling you on some slightly less advanced learning patterns, to get you up to speed?

Elise   Well – I don't need to know about columnar transposition to understand what this is –

Marie-Claude   – Elise. If you are going to be in both departments, then you need a foundation, a framework, an architecture in linguistics. Otherwise. Well, I don't know how to help you.

She walks out, **Elise** *+25 follows trying to reason with her, as their relationship begins to break down.*

Scene Eighteen

+8 years Elise – Lunchtime

Kenny *is putting in a videotape of David Attenborough's* Life on Earth. *We see this play in the corner of the room. It's* **Kenny's** *favourite nature documentary.*

Kenny   Elise. Look – *Life on Earth.* Have you seen it?

Elise   Nope.

Kenny   But you must! It's BBC. I think you'll like it.

Reza *knocks and enters with a tray of lunch.*

Reza   Mr Kenny.

Elise   Selamat siang, Om Reza.

Reza   Elise, lunch!

Kenny   We're just watching *Life on Earth.*

Reza   David Attenborough?

Kenny   Yeah, do you want to join us?

Reza   Ah.

He looks over his shoulder for **Mrs Peters***.*

Kenny   You're more than welcome. Pull up a chair.

Reza   Thank you. Ok.

He does.

Elise. Habiskan sayurnya yah. Supaya kamu makin cepet tingginnya. Dan kalau makan ikan, awas! Banyak tulangnya. [Elise. Finish up your vegetables. So you can grow taller quick. And be careful eating the fish. There's a lot of bones.]

Elise *and* **Reza** *watch* Life on Earth.

After a moment, **Reza** *spots* **Kenny** *listening to music.* It's *'Dancing in the Dark' by Bruce Springsteen.*

Reza *goes over to* **Kenny***.*

Kenny   The Boss. The Boss.

Reza   Who?

Kenny *undoes his headphones.*

Reza   Oh – The Boss!

Kenny   Elise, do you know The Boss?

Kenny *and* **Reza** *both do a little dance move.*

Elise *joins in.*

Kenny   Now *this* is musical education.

In the darkness **Elise +48** *appears.*

They begin to gradually dance more wildly. The lights black out. They all laugh, gradually dancing around with **Reza***'s torch as a disco light. It's joyful, the sort of moment you remember from your childhood.* **Reza** *is dancing on the table.*

Mrs Peters   Mr Robbins! What is going on here? Why is everyone lying on the dirty floor?

Reza! What are you doing in there? Go and do something useful.

Reza *exits sheepishly, leaving* **Kenny** *and* **Elise**.

Mrs Peters (*acutely to* **Kenny**)   Lunchbreak is a time for the children to eat and to rest, not dance around like a baboon.

Kenny   There's still 30 minutes left of lunch.

Mrs Peters   I can hear this racket in my office. You are disturbing me, so I'm assuming you're disturbing the rest of the school.

Kenny   Yes I've been referring to the lesson plans. And she's been responding very we–

Mrs Peters   – Mr Robbins, your approach needs to match our approach to educating our children. Otherwise, I'm afraid you won't be here next week. Elise, have you finished your lunch?

Elise   Yes.

Mrs Peters   Oh good. Someone's doing what they're supposed to do.

She begins to leave. She turns to look at the room.

The mess. It's like a student flat. Clear this up, Mr Robbins.

She leaves slamming the door. **Kenny** *is shocked. But composes himself.*

Kenny   Hey, Elise. Maybe you could draw some of your patterns on the board. Shall we use the whole board? Here, use the chalk. Go wild.

Mr Robbins *goes to find the lesson plan.*

Elise *+48 watches him as he paces around, trying to settle.*

She watches **Elise** *+8 at the whiteboard.*

Scene Nineteen

9 months before Elise III

Ardi *and* **Juliette** *appear from under the set. They look along the wall, continuing to try to find the painting.*

Juliette   Wow. The stalagmites are glistening in the torchlight.

Ardi   I have to get this.

He starts filming the audience with the Super 8. **Juliette** *watches him, admires him.*

Juliette   Shut your eyes.

Ardi   What, why?

Juliette   Just do it.

Ardi *does.*

Juliette   If you listen carefully, you can hear what it was like millions of years ago.

/

Ardi   I love you, Juliette.

Juliette *leans into* **Ardi**, *whispering in his ear.*

Juliette   I know you do.

Come on, where is it then?

Ardi   We're close. We're very near.

Scene Twenty

+43 years – Deciphering II (base camp)

Elise +48 *enters base camp, with her new drawings.* **Marie-Claude** *enters.*

Elise   Marie-Claude. I was watching the guys wave to each other out there, two groups of friends. Waving on different sides of the village to each other. The same gesture, at the same time. How many people are waving at each other, right now all over the world? Thousands, millions?

Marie-Claude   So were the symbols being drawn at the same time as in France? And if so, what and how did they get here, how did the idea get here?

Elise   How long is it for the age on these? The dating?

Marie-Claude   Indra's expecting news from his colleague in Jakarta in the morning.

Elise   It's the number of individual symbols. The variety. Found here. We know they exist in France. In Spain. In Russia. In Peru. In South Africa. These geometric symbols were being created all around the world at the same time, 40,000 years ago. The creative explosion was with abstract symbols, not bison.

Marie-Claude   No, no. We don't know that. You don't know that yet.

Elise   *Mais arrête!* [Please stop!]

Elise *back to the OHP to continue sketching.*

Indra *enters and sits downstage with* **Marie-Claude** *at the table.*

Marie-Claude   Indra, we have to get the water out of the cave.

Indra   Yeah, I spoke to my team already. They are on it.

Marie-Claude   But when?

Indra   Next week, we are looking at it.

Marie-Claude   No, it cannot be next week, it needs to be today, yesterday.

Indra   I understand, MC. My team understands that. Thank you.

Marie-Claude   If it is difficult, I can bring some people over from Paris.

Indra   I am aware.

Marie-Claude   Can I speak with them?

Indra   You want to speak to them?

Marie-Claude   If possible.

/

Indra   MC, we are aware of this. My team have been in there. My team know what they have to do.

Marie-Claude   So, we agree on the problem?

Indra   Of course.

/

Marie-Claude *takes out a shiny-looking document from her bag.*

Indra   What's that?

Marie-Claude   This is what I'm thinking about. For you and your team. Ok I'm thinking if we can seal off the cave. Control the humidity. Install a security system. Like Chauvet. And we need to talk about access, but I would like to talk about going back to the Musée and talk to them. I think they will be interested in helping you to make a research park here. We can also create a tourist attraction here to raise funds. After all, it is their heritage.

Indra *is flicking through the document.*

Indra   This looks like it'd change a lot of things here.

Marie-Claude   Yes, I know but, in our work, we are used at looking at a very big time scale. It is necessary to look beyond a month, six months, a year. So yes. it means possibly we must relocate the village. But the advantages are you have a world-class research centre here, your work here, and you raise the profile for the Indonesian project.

Indra   Are you sure you're French, MC?

Marie-Claude   What?

Indra   Because you sound like the Dutch, 400 years ago.

Marie-Claude   Oh, Indra, this was so successful at the Lascaux cave, the new museum is a fantasti–

Indra   – But this is Indonesia. This is not France. Look. My team and I came up with this.

His proposal is shared.

I wanted to show you, see what you think about it, MC.

This is the first cave found here. There are more. I don't have evidence for that yet. But I know there are. That's important to me.

Marie-Claude   I know.

Indra   These people, they understand the significance of it. They know what is in there and they appreciate it. But I don't think they're going to appreciate you telling them they need to leave their home.

Marie-Claude   Indra, if we don't do this soon then maybe these caves won't be there for their daughters. Or their granddaughters. Just think about this.

Indra   Ok. I'll think about it.

Marie-Claude *leaves* **Indra** *in the gloom of the base-camp light.*

Scene Twenty-One

The astronomy lesson – The planets

Kenny *and* **Elise** *explore the solar system.*

Kenny   Do you know how many planets there are in our solar system?

Elise   Er. Nine?

Kenny   Yes. And do you know the order of the planets?

The lights darken to a blackout. To reveal **Kenny** *holding a glowing yellow ball (lit by a torch). Ping-pong and tennis balls are used as planets in a silent, interactive lesson about the planets.*

The floor rises, to reveal the three panels of the cave one final time.

Scene Twenty-Two

Cave III

Indra *and* **Elise** *+48 are in the cave looking at the panels.*

Elise   Indra, your son Raihan, he's eight, right?

Indra   Yeah.

Elise   Such a good age.

Indra   It is.

Elise   You know when I was his age, I could speak pretty good Bahasa. Yeah, I remember my school in Jakarta. I remember leaving and saying goodbye to my friends and then not much else anymore. It's funny the words that stick all these years later. The words you remember. Our school caretaker, Om Reza was his name.

Reza *appears.*

Reza   *Awas!* Be careful!

He disappears.

Elise   Yeah. He said to me. I remember that word very well.

Indra   Be careful?

Elise   Yeah.

/

Elise   What do you think you're going to do with this place, Indra?

Indra   The way I see this place. This is just the beginning.

Elise   Yeah.

Indra   It is the start of something, you know?

/

Elise   The symbols. Whose are they? I really think it was a group of women. I don't know why.

Who did they leave these for?

Indra   I just don't want to make a mistake, with this place, you know?

Elise   I met the smartest person I've ever known in Jakarta. Someone who helped me realise that you've got to make mistakes to get to the good stuff.

+8 years – silent overlay of planets and stars.

Without really messing up. Without really going on your arse. You don't find the things that really matter.

And I did what I was supposed to a while back, and I have regretted it ever since.

/

Elise   Can you give me a hand for a second. I can't quite reach up there.

*She reaches up to the sky. A photo is taken of one of the symbols on the wall, with **Elise**'s hand for scale.*

Scene Twenty-Three

+25 years – Elise deciding to leave her PhD

Elise   What do you want to be when you grow up?

It's not a particularly interesting question to an eight-year-old, is it?

It's something that we ask in the past tense.

What did you want to be when you were younger?

The tenses, they get confused.

'I wanted to be a train driver.'

'I wanted to be a rock star.'

I wanted to be.

So in my alternative futures, I'm twenty-five and I've tried following my father's dreams, my mother's path, a path offered by Kenny and yet I'm *none* of those things.

I'm a collection of those things. And so much more.

The small exchanges with friends.

Encouragement from the right place.

An accidental brilliant exam result.

I've brought my love of colour, of science, of optics, of history, of language – but aged twenty-five I'm about to be convinced to step back from a PhD. Wow. A PhD. In Palaeoarchaeology.

You already know that wasn't the end for me. You already know I will receive a phone call from Marie-Claude, aged forty-eight, and am allowed to continue that part of my story.

We see **Marie-Claude** *and* **Elise** *+48 revisit their phone call, ahead of the site visit to the cave. There's a sense that the story is cascading in on itself.*

Elise   But I wanted to show you my other paths. To show you just how precious it is to know, to think that you know, what you want to be and then just – to let life guide you.

So – you can see that paths don't have a beginning and an end.

They criss-cross. They create their own patterns.

And eventually, well eventually, the paths cross so much they create a mesh to support you.

The most important thing is that I tried to be brave.

Someone very important told me that once.

Scene Twenty-Four

+26 years – Elise in a PhD supervision, Oxford University – 2003

Marie-Claude *and* **Elise** *+25 sit together.*

Elise   So, my lit review.

Marie-Claude   Ah yes –

Elise   I've read as much as I can across the Anthropological, Linguistic and Archaeological texts. Bateman, Brown, Breuile –

Marie-Claude   – Yeah that's good.

Elise   Yes, but Dr Altneu still insists that I need to go back and do modules in Linguistics, she's even suggesting a whole other MA, so –

Marie-Claude   Yeah, well I've read your literature review, and the writing is ok. But I can sense this is not the area of interest for you. You have a very difficult balance to find. Not to be dismissive of the seminal texts. And there are some key, *huge*, voices missing here. You're missing Lamingham-Perere, Raphael, Reuben-smith, Farquar, I mean I can put a list together for you –

Elise   – No, I hear you. What I'm struggling with is . . . what I feel like is . . . that I'm just wasting my time, reading these perspectives which I wasn't draw to, and things I have a curiosity for –

Marie-Claude   Elise. You know in Archaeology you must make time for the things you don't like because they may hold important for you –

Elise   – Uh-hmm.

Marie-Claude   That is, if you want a future in palaeoarchaeology.

Elise   Of course I do. I just feel like I'm being channelled down a very narrow path. And I have the upmost respect for these writers, but they're not helping me for what I'm curious about. There just aren't enough people who come before me –

Marie-Claude   – Oh!

/

Elise   Does that make any sense? I'm trying to look at this from a non-Eurocentric perspective –

Marie-Claude   – Ok. Ok. You have a very good mind. The proposal is fascinating. But there's 150 years of people – like me – who have been putting in the work before you, and you must do more to earn your place. You cannot start from nothing.

Elise   Um –

Marie-Claude   We don't start from today.

Elise   Yeah. It's just –

Marie-Claude   – It's hard. Yes. You have this great idea. But unless you test your theory, that's all you have. And that is not enough.

/

Right?

/

Elise   If I'm honest with you, it's not something I want to pursue anymore. I think I'm done.

/

Marie-Claude   No, no, no. Wait a minute. Let's take a deep breath for a moment.

/

Your work is good. Your data collection is good. It is thorough. Your idea is fascinating.

Elise   Yeah, but there's no point if it's about the expectation of others. I just wanted to do something I was passionate about, and I don't think I can do that here.

Marie-Claude   I think you're tired.

Elise   I'm not tired.

Marie-Claude   Just take a couple of weeks to think about this.

Elise   No. No, I've explored the various routes, and I don't think there's a way through this for me. In this, in this world.

Marie-Claude   Ok. Well, it will be difficult to, er, to lose you. But you understand, I have no choice but to tell you what I think should do to create this thesis – and have it listened to.

Indra *enters silently speaking to his colleagues in Jakarta.*

Elise   Ok if that's how you want to see it. I just guess I didn't quite know what I was getting myself into.

Scene Twenty-Five

+43 years – Deciphering III (base camp)

Indra *is on the satellite phone looking at the images.*

Indra   *Kamu yakin? Sample B dari ketiga area juga udah diperiksa? Alhamdulillah! Makasih.* [You sure? And the B samples from the three areas have been analysed too? All praise is due to Allah! Thanks.]

He hangs up.

Elise *and* **Marie-Claude** *are stood waiting to hear the news from* **Indra**.

Indra   So – we've had the results back from my team in Jakarta. So, the guys say, from the three samples they took – one of the far-left panel, one on the central panel and on one right panel are dated as follows.

/

So, the left panel, this is 8,000 years old.

Marie-Claude   Wow. That is –

Elise   – Young.

Marie-Claude   Yeah.

/

Indra   The central panel. This panel of symbols is 25,000 years old.

Marie-Claude   Ok, that's the same as Europe. That's what I'd expect.

Indra   And the right panel . . . guess? Anyone.

Marie-Claude   What, tell me, tell us.

Elise   How old, Indra?

/

Indra   The final panel of symbols is just over 43,000 years old. The oldest cave symbols in the world!

They all move away from the laptop. After a moment.

Elise   It's right to left.

Marie-Claude   What?

Elise   Not left to right.

Marie-Claude   It's in age order from right to left.

Indra   Three different ages. Not carried out by one person.

It's a collective across time.

Very Indonesian.

/

Do you think people just see what they want to see?

/

Marie-Claude/Elise   Yes.

Marie-Claude   No. Not you, Elise.

Elise   – I'm no different to anyone else.

Marie-Claude   No, no, Elise, you're the closest anyone has ever got to understanding why.

Elise   I've having this extraordinary feeling. Like I've been talking to my past, present and future all at the same time. I've had these strange flashes. Not back. But inside. Upside down. In reverse and in relief. In all dimensions.

/

Marie-Claude   You know today, when you were with Indra, I *touched* the wall.

Elise   Marie-Claude!

Marie-Claude   Well – I just thought, I've been doing this for thirty years and I'm never allowed to touch the stuff I work with my own hands. So, I just pushed my face to the wall, my cheek.

Elise   I know we saw you. I thought it was very beautiful.

Marie-Claude   Oh God. 8,000, 25000, 43,000 years. All together. Oh my God I must celebrate. No wine though. Ok. I smoke. Yeah, I smoke all of these.

She and **Indra** *both leave,* **Elise** *is sat at the table.*

Elise   So, they're still strange. I like that. We add. And we hope, and we do so, without trying to damage things or hurt people along the way.

Scene Twenty-Six

+8 years – The Rubik's Cube

Kenny *is showing a Rubik's Cube to* **Elise** *+8.*

They all have a Rubik's Cube, we join them mid thought.

Kenny   . . . you want these colours lined up.

He changes tone.

Solving a Rubik's Cube isn't genius. There are just a few things you need to remember. And what you need to remember isn't even that tricky.

The person who invented this, he didn't make it as a puzzle. It was meant to be a tool. For teaching. Erno Rubik. And he taught architecture – do you know what architecture is?

Elise   No.

Kenny   Architecture is how we build things.

Elise   Cool.

Kenny   And this was to teach his students about structure and symmetry.

Kenny *and* **Elise** *+48 are now sat at the table together.* **Elise** *+8 remains on the beanbag.* **Kenny***, for the first time in the story, is talking to* **Elise** *+48.*

Kenny   And he only realised that he'd created a puzzle when he couldn't get back to the beginning. Getting back to the beginning is the puzzle.

You know there are 43 quintillion, and quintillion is 18 zeroes, 43 quintillion possible positions. But only one that's right. It took Rubik a month to solve it for the first time.

When I first got my Rubik's Cube, I tried to work it out on my own, but it was so hard. And frustrating. I kept putting it down and having to walk away. But then someone told me there was a pattern. A pattern of moves that, if you apply in the right order, will solve the puzzle every time.

So, I did. I felt really clever. And talented.

The person who showed me how to do it had been shown by someone else. And that person learnt it from a book. And now I'm showing you.

Being a kid is full of things that don't make sense, Elise. We're born into something that started ages ago and we're playing catch up from the very beginning. When I was kid, I thought the world was very confusing. Bewildering, actually. And I never thought I was any good at anything. Never felt like I knew what to say or what I thought. There's a discomfort around not knowing things, right? When we get something wrong or don't know the answer to a question. But it's not a bad feeling. It's actually a really important feeling. Because it's asks us to be brave. To step outside our comfort zone.

I don't think I stayed in my comfort zone when I was eight as much as I do now.

I just think you should hold on to that.

That interest in what's interesting, whatever that is to you. Just keep being brave. Because you will never fail if you're brave. You literally can't fail if you're brave.

You might not always be the best at things, you might actually be the worst, and I'm pretty bad at some things. But you will never fail if you are brave. It's just not possible.

Scene Twenty-Seven

9 months before Elise IV

Ardi *and* **Juliette** *appear from under the cave. They stop by a wall of limestone.*

Ardi   This is it.

Juliette   Where?

Ardi *gently takes hold of* **Juliette***'s shoulders. Whispering.*

Ardi   Shut your eyes.

Elise *+8 gets up from her reading on the beanbag. She holds her handprint out across towards her parents.*

Juliette   Can I open them now?

Ardi   Open your eyes now.

Elise*'s handprint is on the wall of the cave. They find the little handprint in a headtorch.*

Juliette *takes an intake of breath. As if you've seen the most beautiful artwork.*

Ardi*, whispering, very gently.*

Ardi   You know what I thought when I first saw it?

Juliette   What?

/

Ardi   How . . . how did a child's handprint get so high?

/

Juliette *looks at* **Ardi** *considering how best to answer the question.*

Juliette   Well. You'd lift the child up.

/

Ardi   What do you mean?

Juliette   You'd lift *our* child up.

Lights fade on stage. The headtorch is switched off.

Traversing 40,000 years, we see **Juliette** *and* **Ardi** *in silhouette with their daughter* **Elise** *in the shadows of the theatre.*

The music soars. The lights fade. A handprint floating in the air is the only image left visible.